Preparing for Year End in Accounts Payable: A 60-Minute Guidebook

Mary S. Schaeffer

Accounts Payable Now & Tomorrow

MARY S. SCHAEFFER

ISBN: 978-0615881515

Table of Contents

Preface   4

Chapter 1: The Start of the Year-End Close
Process   5

Chapter 2: Operational Issues: Department
Operations   14

Chapter 3: Operational Issues: Expense
Reimbursements   30

Chapter 4: Operational Issues:
            Year-End Specific   39

Chapter 5: Form 1099 Reporting Issues   46

Chapter 6: The Finishing Touches   57

Appendices

    Glossary   66
    Index   68
    Review Questions Explained   70
    Excerpt from:101 Best Practices
        for Accounts Payable   84
    Articles from Sample issue of Accounts
    Payable Now & Tomorrow newsletter   88
    About the Author   121
    About AP Now   122

Preface

Whether an organization's fiscal year-end coincides with the calendar year-end or not, it inevitably brings additional work and stress. This is especially true in accounts payable. Without proper attention, invoices that arrived weeks and months earlier have a way of suddenly appearing increasing the workload—at the least convenient time. There's also the issue of traveling employees who sit for months on expense reimbursement reports and suddenly come to life when their bosses prod them to get their reporting done.

While the extra work is not likely to go away, effectively and intelligently dealing with the process can make a serious dent in the stress level. This quick-read publication is designed to help readers develop effective strategies to make the year-end process run as smoothly as possible in accounts payable.

Chapter 1:
The Start of the Year-End Close Process

Year-end may come at different times for different organizations. For the purposes of this discussion we are referring to the end of the fiscal year, not the end of the calendar year, although for many, they are the same.

Those organizations whose fiscal year-end close coincides with the end of the calendar year may also be handling employee evaluations at the same time. Those managers really have their hands full. Although employee evaluations are very important, they are not included in this discussion for they are more an HR issue than an accounting matter.

What AP Needs to Do to Get Ready for the Year-End Close

The year-end close is a lot of extra work. It

usually can run smoother than it does, but that takes some advance preparation, planning, scheduling and revamping based on last year's performance and any new requirements your organization might have. What follows is a 15-step plan to help get your accounts payable department ready for the close. It is possible that not all the steps will be applicable to your firm.

1. Budget process. If at all possible, submit estimates and then review final budget before the year-end process starts. While the timeframe for the budget process is usually beyond the control of the accounts payable department, the initial submission can be prepared early, regardless of the company's timeframe.

2. Annual performance reviews are often completed at year-end. The salary component, at least as far as the amount for the entire department, may be part of the budget process. If at all possible, schedule performance reviews early in the month or separate them completely from year end.

3. If you print your own Form 1099s, order the forms as early as possible. Order slightly more than you need to accommodate errors. But, don't get carried away and order a supply for several years. If the IRS changes the

format, the stock you ordered will be worthless.

4. Go through paper files and pull files not used on a regular basis and send them to long term cold storage or have them scanned. Of course, front-end scanning is a much more efficient use of resources, eliminating this task completely from your year-end schedule.

5. If you have many paper files and need to set up new files for the upcoming year, order new files and labels, where appropriate. Obviously, if you only have a few files to add each year, this step won't be necessary.

6. Produce your year-end schedule and share with all who are affected. (See related article on details for preparing the schedule).

7. Request internal audits for the upcoming year for areas you think might need review. Now many people reading this are probably shaking their heads in disbelief but that is missing the big picture. If you have an area you know has weak controls and have run into some resistance from management on making changes, invite the auditors in for a visit. In all likelihood, they will make the same

recommendations as you and that will be one less battle for you to fight.

8. Follow up on un-cashed checks to determine if they should be reversed or moved to unclaimed property reserve fund. This is required due diligence by the states and you'll have to do it anyway at some point. So, why not do it before year end and get those un-cashed checks off the books, one way or the other.

9. Complete statement audits of as many suppliers as possible identifying all open credits. But don't only identify them, reclaim them before the books are closed. You can either do this by applying the credits to outstanding invoices or requesting a check for the outstanding amount. Request a check if you have no outstanding invoices and are not likely to order from this vendor in the near future. Don't let the vendor tell you the credits must be used against an open order, as a few unscrupulous vendors do in an attempt to force an order. That is ridiculous. The money belongs to your organization and you have every right to reclaim it.

10. Send a last call notice to all travelers reminding them of the last cut-off date for expense reimbursements for the fiscal year. While this may seem like an

unnecessary step, in an automated environment it does not take a lot of time or effort. It is worth it if you avoid the aggravation of even one employee who submits late and then demands reimbursement to pay a looming credit card bill.

11. Send a last call reminder to all employees who submit invoices for payment reminding them of the last cut-off date for invoices to be submitted for payment. This is especially important because some of your vendors with similar fiscal year-ends will need to have monies owed remitted before the year-end. Again, you can avoid some ugly confrontations by reminding everyone of the cut-off date.

12. Verify accruals and coordinate with other departments if accounts payable only produces part of the accrual for outstanding invoices.

13. Resolve issues on all outstanding discrepant invoices. Clearly, this is easier said than done but it is important. Discrepant invoices should be included in accruals but are often overlooked. Year-end is also a good time to finally address those invoices that have hung around for months.

14. Review notes from last year's close to identify potential problem spots and fix them to avoid similar problems. Also, you can use this information when establishing due dates on this year's calendar.

15. Set up a new year-end calendar reflecting the work completed in the accounts payable department along with realistic cut-off and completion dates for the current fiscal year based on requirements and last year's experiences.

While there's probably nothing that can guarantee a stress-free year-end close, following the steps listed above is a good step towards eliminating many of the unnecessary headaches.

This Year Will Be Different: Getting Ready for Year End

By the end of January were you in need of a few weeks on a Caribbean beach? Were your nerves shot from dealing with staff, employees outside the department, independent contractors, auditors and vendors? Did you long for a good night's sleep and some quiet? Did you swear that this year-end would be different and you'd be prepared? Have you done anything to address that promise? Now is the time to get ready. Now is the time to prepare.

1) **Vacations**. It is unfortunate that the holidays coincide with the busiest time of

the work year in a large number of organizations. It's the time when most of the employees want time off and most AP managers need to staff for overtime; a guarantee of conflict. Address the issue now. Survey your staff about their plans and devise the best schedule you can that will address their needs and yours. Take this off December's plate but anticipate some grumbling.

2) **To-Do List**. Prepare your list of tasks that will have to be accomplished along with approximate dates as to when things must be finished. If you do this each year, you can simply take last year's list and add to it.

3) **1099s**. If you need to order forms, make sure you do so. If you want to sign your staff up for either one-day training or webinars on this topic, do it now. There are a number of good resources in this arena. Communicate with the staff. Let them know you are thinking about them.

4) **Morale**. If there is to be a year-end party, start planning now. The holidays are hard for many people. Combine this with extra work and you've got a recipe for trouble. Let the staff know you are thinking of them. The year-end party is just one way to address their needs.

5) **Invoices**. Start looking at your disputed invoices and get as many of those disputes resolved and the invoices processed as possible.

6) **Reviews**. Many organizations review all employees at year end. Talk adding fuel to an already stressful situation. Begin now to prepare, collecting the information you need about who has done what. But, be realistic. Expect a certain number of your employees to be disappointed in their reviews. You will never please everyone, especially if budgets are tight.

7) **Budget** for education. When the budget is done, make sure you get some money for staff education—and then spend it on the staff. Let them know you are concerned about their future and careers.

While nothing can guarantee a stress-free year end, addressing these issues should help reduce the tension in your accounts payable department.

Review Questions Chapter 1

1) To get ready for year-end, which of the following tasks should be completed?

- A. If you print your own 1099s, order the forms early
- B. Encourage employees to take vacation time as they wish for morale purposes
- C. Ignore disputed invoices as there is too much other work to be done at year end
- D. Begin planning for new projects for next year

2) With regards to un-cashed checks that have been outstanding for a long time, which action should be taken at year-end?

- A. They should be written off to miscellaneous income
- B. They should be followed up on to determine if they should be reversed
- C. They should voided
- D. They should be ignored; eventually they will be cashed

Explanations of the correct responses to the review questions are available at the end of the book starting on page 71.

Chapter 2:
Operational Issues: Department Operations

The Last Check Run: A Five Step Plan to Make the Last Run Really the Last Run

Possibly one of the most stressful issues at the fiscal year end is making sure all checks that need to be cut within the fiscal year are included in that last run. The matter is compounded by the fact that once the run is complete, no checks can be issued within the fiscal year and sometimes within the first few days of the new fiscal year. Yet, it seems almost without exception, the minute the run is complete, check requests come seemingly out of nowhere that must be handled. What can you do to minimize the chances of this happening in your organization? The following action plan will help.

1) Plan wisely. Set the date for that last run as late in the month as possible. While it is tempting to make it earlier so other issues can be attended to, the longer the timeframe when no

checks can be issued, the more likely they are to appear. So, when creating your year-end schedule, think long and hard about the date for your last check run and then make it as late as possible.

2) Give plenty of notice. Make sure anyone who might possibly need to request a check, be it to pay an invoice or for some other special reason, knows the cut-off date for submitting their request. And, publicize this date long in advance so no one can complain that they didn't have enough time to get their request in. You can see a sample notice in the accompanying box.

3) Tell them and then tell them again. Don't rely on one e-mail to notify the staff of the date of the last check run. Send out an initial schedule, say a month before the end of the fiscal year end, and then remind them during the period.

4) Give special attention to known laggards. If you've got employees who are notoriously bad meeting deadlines, send them a personalized message reminding them of the deadline a week before the end of the fiscal year end. Include in this "special" mailing anyone who brought items in for payment after the cut-off date last year. And, if anyone tries to request a payment after the cut-off date this year, make a note of it so they can get the special notice next year.

5) Send out a last call notice. Two to three

days before the cut-off date, send out an e-mail blast to everyone in the company reminding them they only have two days to submit invoices or check requests for the current fiscal year.

Subject Line: Important Notice: Last Check Run

The final check run of the year will be on [fill in the date]. Accounts payable must receive all approved invoices, check requests and expense reimbursement requests by [fill in the date] in order to have a check cut as part of that run. The next check run will be on [fill in the date].

Handling Discrepant and Outstanding Invoices at Year End

Most organizations make an attempt to clean up their books before the fiscal year-end. Clearly this includes your vendors. While discrepant invoices should always be worked on and resolved as quickly as possible, we know that occasionally this does not happen. They become a special issue at year-end. We'll take a look at why this is such a big issue and what you can do about it.

Why Discrepant Invoices Are a Year-End Issue

Your suppliers' collection folks are encouraged to collect as many outstanding invoices as possible while their AR folks are busy cleaning up their accounts, as well. This means getting rid of old outstanding credits as well as resolving discrepancies on outstanding invoices. While this is not an article on accruals, we should point out that discrepant invoices do need to be included in accrual calculations; so reducing their number makes that process a little smoother as well.

Some will contact the customer but others see an easier way. If you have an open credit (possibly one you know nothing about) the vendor may decide to use that open credit to clear out the discrepant invoice. They are not doing this to be mean; they simply are trying to clean up the books. Some may even feel they are doing you a favor – even though your organization will not really see it that way.

The best way to avoid this problem is to make sure all discrepant invoices are resolved expeditiously. Of course, this is easier said than done.

Resolving Discrepant Invoices: The Basics

The sooner an invoice discrepancy is resolved, the more likely it is that all parties will remember the details. Time is not an asset when it comes to resolving problems. Managers should track all outstanding invoices and regularly follow up with the person responsible for resolving the issue. Most often, this is the invoice processor.

Tracking and publishing statistics around outstanding invoices is one strategy some organizations take to encourage processors to get invoices issues resolved quickly. In fact, in some places it is a contest as everyone strives not to be the processor with the oldest invoice as well as the one with the most unresolved invoice issues.

Probably the best way to reduce the number of invoice disputes is to identify common causes for discrepancies. This means not only tracking discrepancies but also identifying the problem when the issues are resolved. It also means tracking everyone involved to determine if one particular vendor, or one purchaser, or one processor is at the root of the common problem. In any of these cases a frank discussion and/or additional training should put a dent in the number of discrepancies arising from this particular facet.

Of course, for this to work, it means someone has to keep track of all the details and then take the time to analyze the metrics. This is a good project to be completed in the summer or perhaps early fall before year-end rolls around (at least for those who have a fiscal year-end that coincides with the end of the calendar year.

Some choose to start their monitoring at the beginning of the new fiscal year so the next close won't include so many discrepant invoices.

While there will always be legitimate reasons for discrepancies between what the customer expects to pay and the invoice presented by the vendor, the number of these annoyances can be kept to a minimum, if everyone involved does what they are supposed to do. This means presenting a clean purchase order, a receiving department that closely checks what is shipped against the packing slip, and of course, a purchasing staff that reviews invoices before approving them for payment. But even with everyone playing their part, discrepancies will arise and this is the place where accounts payable can add real value.

Handling Invoices at Year End: Getting Them into the Correct Fiscal Year

One of our readers asked how invoices are handled at fiscal yearend. She specifically wanted to know how to make sure how to get all invoices entered for the current fiscal year without entering invoices that should be part of the following year. We asked readers of our weekly e-zine about this and were flooded with responses. To a large degree, how this task is handled will depend on the capabilities of the accounting software. Some can handle it but many can't. Here are the best explanations we received.

The Manual Approach

1) Before we upgraded our financial software, we used to have to separate the invoices by period manually. We kept a manual file labeled Year XXXX and put the invoices into

that folder that related to the next year. On the first day we are able to access the new year in the software, we then entered all of the invoices in this folder. Now, our software allows us to post invoices into the Payables module of the current year even though the financial module of the prior year is still open.

2) We actually look at each invoice and determine which period it belongs in. If we receive an invoice in December for a future period and it needs to be paid in December, we code it to a prepaid account, then relieve the prepaid account in January or over the period of time the invoice pertains. We hold open our year end for a couple of weeks, however, if something monetary comes along after that period of time, we accrue it into the month of December. If the invoice does not need to be entered and paid until January, we wait until the first of January to key it into our system.

3) After having invoices approved for payment, we sort them into two piles, one with year ending date of end of fiscal year and before, and one pile with the beginning date of the new fiscal year. We then process one pile at a time. Of course, it's usually about 30 days that care must be taken to watch for the prior fiscal invoices, but eventually, they all are processed.

4) Our challenge is with the Non-PO items. The day before and the day of closing (after Jan 1st), we instruct our processors to post all the

Non-PO invoices first, changing the period end date when necessary.

The Fiscal Year Approach

1) We also struggle with year-end invoices. In order to report as accurately as possible, we look at the date on the invoice that indicates when the goods were shipped. Then we calculate whether we received the goods in that fiscal year. If we did, we enter it as an old year invoice. If we did not physically receive the goods in the old fiscal year, we enter the invoice in the new fiscal year. We do this regardless of the date on the invoice. We "own the goods" when they arrive at our door (FOB Destination) so all invoices are figured by the same method. Some invoices are more difficult to estimate receipt date than others but for the most part this is the best way we have come up with for old year/new year ambiguity.

2) Our organization (public) determines the FY year based on the date of the requisition, which would indicate what FY the expense is being charged to. However, if the person requisitioning, jumps the gun and orders product/services prior to the submission of proper documents and they are received in the prior fiscal, it would be charged to the prior FY regardless of their desires.

3)   As fiscal year end approaches, Accounts Payable and the Controller's Office get together and come up with invoicing parameters. We backdate the transaction date to the previous fiscal year for the first ten days of the new fiscal year, allowing for all invoices regardless of dollar amount to be entered into the appropriate year. Then each week we gradually raise the dollar threshold for which invoices we will backdate the transaction date in order to hit the appropriate fiscal year. We do this for about five weeks and then the previous fiscal year is closed for Accounts Payable. Anything that has a huge dollar value would need to be done so through the Controller's Office and a journal voucher.

4)   We don't handle invoices any differently at year end; they are processed as they come across our desk and fall into whatever month we are in that day. Our largest division runs reports every month to reclassify large dollar expenses into the appropriate month if needed. It helps to be very current with invoice processing (processing invoices as they come in, or within a day or so). If we do happen to see an invoice is for the future fiscal year we wait to process it when the new year is open, but this is less than a handful of invoices.

As you can see, there is no easy solution to this problem. Hopefully one of these solutions will work for your organization.

An 8 Step Plan: Dealing with Vendor Credits

Vendor credits are one of those dirty little secrets few organizations like to talk about. Vendor credits are those amounts of money that represent an overpayment and are held on the vendors' books. They arise from a myriad of reasons including, but not limited to:

- Returns

- Defective products

- Quantity discounts

- Volume rebates

- Simple overpayments and duplicate payments

What's The Problem?

When vendor credits are created most suppliers take one of the following courses of action:

1) They notify the customer, usually by issuing a credit memo or,

2) They do nothing.

If they issue a credit memo, it may or may not get to accounts payable. Often it is sent to purchasing. When that happens, the credit memo may be forwarded to accounts payable or it may be tossed in the garbage. Even if it is sent to accounts payable, more than occasionally, either nothing happens with it or the processor doesn't recognize it and treats it as an invoice. And of course, if the supplier does nothing, it is difficult for the customer to know of the credits.

At the end of the day, whatever the reason, many credits sit on the vendors' books unclaimed by their rightful owners. As year-end approaches, this can be a real problem. Here's why.

Accounts receivable professionals will attempt to "clean up" their accounts towards the end of their fiscal year. They also sometimes do this at the end of each quarter. They'll look at the open credits on an account and look for outstanding fees (think late fees that you don't pay) or unauthorized deductions (unearned early pay discounts and other deductions not approved by the vendor) and they'll clean up the books, using the open credits to eliminate the fees and deductions. They'll also use them to pay off disputed invoices. Many do this with the best of intentions. And then there are a few devious vendors who just take the open credits into miscellaneous income.

Clearly, if you don't take some actions to reclaim your open vendor credits, a good portion of them will be lost.

The Unclaimed Property Issue

Some reading this may rightly be thinking that open credits are unclaimed property and should be turned over to the states at the appropriate time. And, if you are thinking this you are 100% correct. If you are thinking that you'll just recover your organization's money when it is turned over to the states, you might want to reconsider.

For starters, as discussed above, the vendor credits have a way of evaporating. So, by the time the credits should be turned over, many have evaporated. This of course, assumes the vendor complies with unclaimed property rules. Experts estimate that only one-third of all organizations who should comply actually do. So, your open credits would have to be with an organization that reported unclaimed property and knew it was supposed to include open credits in that reporting.

And finally, there is the delicate issue trying to reclaim unclaimed property from the state, if you are not reporting yourself. Of course, everyone is urged to report and remit as is required by law. But, if your organization is not up to date on its reporting obligations, the last thing you would want to do would be to wave a red flag in front of the states by trying to recover your unclaimed property.

The reality is that in the last few years, many of the states have started checking their records when a comply tries to recover property. If the company is not in compliance it is likely it will find itself scheduled for an audit. So, get in compliance before trying to recover property.

Recovering All Your Open Credits

The first move in the recovery process is to recognize this issue. The following steps should help you recover most, if not all, of your outstanding open credits.

1) Review all accounts at least once a year. Begin by requesting the vendor send a statement showing all open activity. Make sure the vendor understands you want credits included. Otherwise, some may take advantage of the nasty feature in their software that allows them to suppress vendor credits when printing statements. Every account should be reviewed at least once a year, as credits are not always where you think they'd be.

2) Identify those accounts with significant recoveries and schedule them for quarterly reviews. There's no sense leaving your funds sitting any longer than necessary. Quarterly reviews will help. Some even get monthly statements, if credit experience warrants it.

3) Once the credits have been identified either request funds be returned or ask for a credit memo. Make sure you staff on top of this issue, tracking credits requested and credits used. Some simply take the credit.

4) Re-solicit those vendors who have not supplied recent statements. Just because you ask

for the statements, doesn't mean all vendors will comply. Politely, but firmly, remind vendors who haven't sent copies of requested statements that you are waiting for them. Realistically though, be aware that it is unlikely you'll get 100% of the statements you request, no matter how persistent you are.

5) Set up a regular schedule for requesting statements (and reviewing them) as part of your accounts payable procedures. It's not enough to request and receive the statements; the value comes in reviewing them and recovering the funds owed your organization.

6) Keep track of all your recoveries, along with the reasons the credits were created in the first place. This information is critical to plugging the gaps in your processes.

7) Analyze the data related to your recoveries to determine where you can tighten your processes to ensure future credits are not created. It's not enough to simply recover your open credits; you want to stop them from being created, where possible. It's probably not possible to completely eliminate them, but you can make a serious dent in them by studying the issues that lead to their creation.

8) Periodically review new data to identify new places where you may have weaknesses in your processes that result in the creation of vendor credits. The analytical process is not a

one-shot project but one that should be repeated every year or two to identify new problem spots.

Concluding Thoughts

This is not a simple project. It is something that needs to be done on a regular basis and these funds have a direct impact on the profitability of your organization. Don't have adequate resources to handle this task? Consider outsourcing it to a firm that specializes in statement review and recoveries.

Review Questions – Chapter 2

1.   At year-end, to ensure a smooth a close as possible, who should be sent special notices to remind them of deadlines?

A.   All vice presidents
B.   Known laggards
C.   The purchasing manager
D.   The sales manager

2.   What is the best way to reduce the number of discrepant invoices?

A.   Refuse to handle discrepant invoices throwing the problem back to the vendor
B.   Stop doing business with those vendors who have the most discrepancies
C.   Ignore all discrepancies and pay what you think is correct
D.   Identify common root causes and eliminate them

3.   Vendor statements should be requested and reviewed how frequently?

A.   Never, suppliers automatically write checks for open credits
B.   At least once a year, if not more frequently
C.   Every two or three years
D.   Daily

Explanations of the correct responses to the review questions are available at the end of the book starting on page 71.

Chapter 3:
Operational Issues: Expense Reimbursements

Dealing with The Year-End Expense Reimbursement Surge

One of the many "surprises" that come out of the woodwork at year-end is the issue of the T&E laggards. These are those folks who somehow never have time to do their expense reports. When the message goes out that all reports for the current fiscal year must be turned in by a certain date, they get busy.

So why don't these employees turn their expense reports in as they are supposed to? The answer is quite simple. They are tardy because their organizations allow it. Like most other employees they are overworked and there is always something more important to be done. They quickly learn that if they ignore the reminders that the Accounts Payable manager sent, nothing happened. If the company pays the credit card bill they will become pros at charging most of their expenses and not have a huge financial incentive to complete their reports. If the organization offers cash advances to traveling employees, the situation is even worse.

The moral of this story is that for some employees there have to be consequences for not turning in their reports on time; otherwise they won't—even honorable employees who have the best of intentions. It's only at year-end, just at the time when accounts payable already has its hands full, that these laggards get their expense reports turned in—and usually at the very last minute.

Tough Tactics to Get T&E Reports Submitted On Time!

Anyone involved in T&E processing for more than a few months becomes painfully aware that it is difficult to get certain employees to submit their T&E reimbursement forms on a timely basis. Let's face it, filling out a T&E report and attaching all those annoying receipts is not a whole lot of fun. The problem is exacerbated in those organizations where the company pays the credit card bill. There, employees have little incentive to get their reports turned in on time. Or do they? AP Now asked readers about this issue in a recent survey. Here are some tactics they use with great success:

- Submit a report each month to the president of the company. It contains the employees' names and receipt dates.

- Have an e-mail go out under the president's name (or that of some other high-level executive) asking for the late reports. Most people only have to get this note once.

- Inform senior managers and supervisors of late or missing reports.

- Do not provide any reimbursements to employees who have outstanding expense reports.

- Deactivate the credit cards until required documentation is submitted.

- Require that the employee pay all late credit card charges. Actually, the organization that uses this approach gives the employees one pass, paying the charges the first time.

- Credit card payment is not made until T&E report is received.

- Send correspondence to the employee with escalations to increasing levels of management if the employee does not resolve the matter.

- Do not provide cash advances. If the company insists on offering them to traveling employees, restrict this privilege to those who are not late with their reports.

- If an employee receives an advance and does not submit a report within 30 days, the employee's manager is called in to explain to the division director.

Are you cringing reading this? Yes, the tactics described are harsh. But getting expense reports submitted on time is important and sometimes it takes a tough approach to get the matter resolved.

Less Harsh Methods of Getting the Laggards to Turn in Reports on Time

Getting reports turned in on time is an issue for certain Accounts Payable departments. You can begin by spelling out the corporate expectations in the policy. This sets the stage and can make the timing a policy-compliance issue. If your organization is not willing to take the steps described in the previous section—and many aren't—try some of these less draconian tactics:

- Send out a reminder e-mail to everyone at your company who travels several days before your check run cutoff, reminding all travelers of your reimbursement deadlines.

- Give every traveler one Get-Out-of-Jail-Free card. This will enable them to get a last-minute reimbursement, if they have the necessary documentation approved. While this will guarantee a certain number of Rush checks, it serves notice that each traveler will be accommodated only once. This is useful if you are at a company that will require you to issue the Rush check. If you want to have a very strict policy of never reimbursing people outside the normal check production cycle, do not use this technique.

- Provide each new employee with your policy and procedures regarding T&E reimbursement. Try and narrow it down to a one-page cheat sheet. Otherwise, they are unlikely to read it.

- Give your one-page cheat sheet to any employee who requests a last-minute reimbursement along with their check.

- Refuse to give cash advances to the traveling employee until the prior advance has been accounted for (assuming you give cash advances in the first place).

- Every problem presents an opportunity and don't overlook this one: If you are trying to convert everyone to automated clearinghouse (ACH) reimbursements, limit your last-minute accommodations to payment via the ACH. If you can get away with it, insist that the employee continue to be reimbursed that way.

Approvals: Dealing with the Foot-Dragging Manager

The laggard problem does not always lie with the employee. Sometimes it's with the approving manager. Most of the time, when a manager does not approve his or her employees' T&E expense reports, it is simply because the manager has too many other things to do.

Occasionally it is something else. If your AP staff is not careful, they can find themselves drawn into an ongoing battle between a boss and a subordinate. This can happen when the boss and the subordinate, for whatever reason, are not getting along. One of the ways the boss retaliates is to not approve the T&E expense report. If the employee needs the funds to pay her credit card, she is put in an awkward position. Often, in these circumstances, she will try and get the AP department to act as the middleperson. This is not what you are paying the Accounts Payable staff for and it is a lose-lose situation for them.

Taking Action

The reason for the lack of approval is not the concern for the person handling the T&E expense process. It should not become his or her problem. There are several ways that the staff can deal with this issue. Begin by ignoring whatever problems may be going on between the boss and the subordinate, if that is an issue. If you have sent out a reminder e-mail to employees about their T&E reports and several state that the reports have been submitted but their managers have not yet approved them, immediately send a memorandum e-mail to the approvers reminding them of the upcoming cutoff dates.

After a while you will get to know who are the regulars, when it comes to forgetting to approve reports. Automatically send them a reminder e-mail notice. Some professionals automatically send all approvers such a reminder each payment cycle. There is one thing you should keep in mind about these e-mails. After a while, the employees will already know what your e-mails say. If they are gently nagging ones, as these reminders tend to be, the staff won't open them.

So, make sure the information in the subject line conveys your message. The message line could say something like: June 12: Cutoff date for T&E reimbursements. While this is certainly not worthy of any literary award, it will convey the needed information to your employees and approvers. And, since they haven't opened the e-mail, the message will stand out because it will remain bolded in many systems.

If you are sending reminder e-mails to approvers, copy the employee on the message. That way the employee can put some pressure on the manager and increase the odds of your receiving the approved report within your timeframe.

Finally, if you cannot get the necessary approval, escalate it to the approver's boss. While this tactic is not likely to win many friends, it is extremely effective. Few people have to do it more than once. You can clearly state your time requirements for escalation in your T&E policy. In this way, no one can claim you blindsided them. If you want, information about potential escalations can be included in reminder e-mails.

Review Questions – Chapter 3

1. What is the main reason some employees turn in their expense reports late?

A. Their companies allow them to do so, despite written policies
B. They have too much work to do
C. Companies don't care when employees turn in their expense reports
D. Companies encourage employees to turn in their expense reports late

2. Which of the following tactics will encourage employees to turn their expense reports on time?

A. Refuse to pay all late fees for employees
B. Make credit card payments for employees, even if expense report has not been received
C. Give cash advances
D. Never remind employees or their supervisors of late expense reports

Explanations of the correct responses to the review questions are available at the end of the book starting on page 71.

Chapter 4:
Operational Issues: Year-End Specific

The Year End Calendar:
A Tool for Improvement as Well as Process

A Year End calendar can serve as the guiding document towards a smoother close. Used properly, it can also serve as a tool to help organizations re-engineer their year-end processes to make the process more efficient. While most organizations create a year-end schedule, not all of them get as much out of them as they could. Let's take a look at what a calendar should include and some ways to get the most out of the process.

Components of the Calendar

Simply put, the calendar will contain the following information:

- Due Date
- Action Required
- Person/Department Responsible
- Date Action Completed

- Comments/Notes

There may be a calendar for the entire accounting function and a separate one for the accounts payable function or there may just be one master calendar.

Using the Calendar

The calendar should be a document that is not static. Ideally, it will be completed in the form of an Excel spreadsheet for easy sorting, when needed. For example, you might sort the master calendar into departmental groups. Typically, it is arranged in due date order – but again, if it is in an Excel spreadsheet each user can sort it as suits their requirements best.

Once the year-end process has started, don't overlook the notes and comments field. As you finish each of your requirements, note the date they were finished as well as any comments you might have. If you encountered a problem include that. If you have a solution that might make it work easier next year, include that as well. Don't hope you'll remember it next year – write it down!

When the year-end tasks are finally completed, don't delete the file. Save it for next year.

Planning for the Next Close

The first step when planning for the close should be to pull out last year's calendar with all the notes you made. Begin by looking to see if your group made all its due dates. If you missed any, were there extenuating circumstances that caused you to miss the due date or are you likely to be in the same boat this year. If it looks like you'll need extra time, request it before the schedule is published. Otherwise, you'll miss the due date and it will reflect poorly on the department.

Conversely, if you had certain tasks finished early, you might consider offering to move your due date closer to the close by a day or two. If you are wondering why you would do this, consider the impact of your move on others. Would it make it easier for them to do their portion of the close?

Review the responsibility column. Have you had any changes either in staff or in how work is completed that might require a change to this column? If so, report it before the report is published.

Finally, take a close look at the comments you made last year to determine what changes need to be made both to the calendar and to how your group will operate.

By reviewing this report early, ideally a month or two before anyone even starts thinking about the close, you will be best positioned to have the changes made you need. This way, the accounts payable department will come out looking like a star when the close is complete.

Handling Accruals in Accounts Payable

Most accounts payable departments prepare accruals at the end of each fiscal period. Some do it at the end of each month. Often organizations have been doing it for so long; no one gives it a second thought. But, that is not a great way to approach any function, especially one that affects the financial information, used by management to make important decisions regarding the future of organization. In this piece, we look at what we mean by accruals, why they are so important and a game plan for creating accurate accruals for your organization.

The Concept

The goal of the fiscal period accrual process is to record expenses and related liabilities in the period in which they were incurred. When it comes to accounts payable, accruals reflect the amount of money the company has committed (or is obligated) to pay in the future. Typically, this is represented by invoices that have not been paid, funds owed for goods that have been received but not yet billed for, interest that is owed but not paid for the period and any similar obligations. At the end of the fiscal period, the organization needs to make sure expenses are recorded for all goods or services you have received during the year.

Budgeted items that have not yet been spent are not included when calculating accruals. Those reading this probably realize that not all the information needed to calculate an accurate accrual will lie in accounts payable. It is often necessary to work with purchasing and other departments to collect all accrual information.

Why Accruals Matter

Accruals are important for a number of reasons. They help organization produce more accurate financial statements. This in turn helps them make more realistic business decisions as they are working from accurate numbers. They won't be surprised when a large unexpected expense pops up in the new fiscal period.

While all this is true, there is one other issue to keep in mind. Accruals are often estimates and as such are not always accurate.

The Accrual Process in Accounts Payable

An entry, called an accrual, should be recorded when a good or service has been received in the current fiscal period but will not be paid for prior to fiscal period-end. This entry debits an expense for the related amount and credits accounts payable on our balance sheet.

An entry should be recorded when a bill has been paid in the current fiscal period for a good or service that will not be received until the next fiscal period. This entry records a prepaid expense; it debits a prepaid expense object code on the balance sheet and credits the expense object code from which the bill was paid.

To ensure correct entries are created, work with other departments (mainly purchasing) to collect all invoices they may be holding. Employees who travel should also be reminded to get their expense reports submitted.

Review open purchase orders to determine if the goods have been received but the invoice has not yet arrived. Also, you might set a threshold under which outstanding items are not accrued for.

The accrual process is not perfect but everyone should attempt to come as close as possible to an accurate figure.

Review Questions – Chapter 4

1. Why is it important to keep notes on problems encountered during the close?

A. It is required by GAAP
B. To apportion blame afterwards
C. To plan on how to avoid the problem next year
D. To plan how to get another department to do the task next year

2. Why are accruals so important?

A. They are necessary for tax reasons
B. They are needed for legal reasons
C. They help decide staffing requirements for the coming fiscal year
D. To help give an accurate financial picture of the organization

Explanations of the correct responses to the review questions are available at the end of the book starting on page 71.

Chapter 5:
Form 1099 Reporting Issues

A Ten Step Plan to Get Any Organization Ready In Compliance with the Form 1099 Reporting Rules

Whether you are getting ready to comply with the 1099 rules or just implementing best practices in your current 1099 procedures the process is the same. Those already using best practices in this area are prepared. After all, what's the big deal? All you have to do is collect, track and verify. Of course those responsible for this task know all too well, collecting W-9s, tracking the process and verifying that the information provided using the IRS TIN Matching program is not as easy as it sounds.

Before You Can Start Your Process

Step 1: Cleanse the master vendor file focusing on:

- Eliminating duplicate vendors
- Deactivating inactive vendors

- Getting a good mailing address, in addition to the bank lock box address many have in their Remit to field.

Step 2: Set up a methodology for tracking the receipt of W-9s. This can be done in your master vendor file, your ERP system or elsewhere. The important issue is that as part of your invoice processing a check be done to ensure a good W-9 has been received. Ideally, this will be automated with your system refusing to schedule the invoice for payment without the requisite TIN information.

Step 3: Sign up to use the IRS TIN Matching program.

Collecting the TIN Information

Step 4: To update your records if you have not collected W-9s in the past, send out letters and/or emails requesting W-9s. Make is easy for your vendors. Let them respond by mail, fax or email.

Step 5: Request a W-9 from new vendors, ideally before the PO is issued but definitely before a payment is made.

Step 6: When new orders are to be placed with existing vendors who have not supplied W-9s, request one. Ideally the vendor should be notified at the time the order is contemplated that the W-9 is required and the PO will not be issued until the W-9 has been received.

Tracking Your TIN Collection Efforts

Step 7: Track the receipt of the W-9s.

Step 8: Follow up with those who do not respond.

Verifying Your TIN Data

Step 9: Run information provided on the W-9through the IRS TIN Matching Program before making the payment.

Step 10: Follow up with any vendor whose data was rejected

Concluding Thoughts

This is a process that best practice organizations have been using. For them it is nothing new. Make it a standard part of your invoice processing procedures regardless of what action Congress takes.

Form 1099-MISC: Filing for an Extension

Despite the fact that everyone knows well in advance of the due date when Information Returns are due, many organizations still can't seem to get the necessary information together and sent to the IRS by the due date. They need an extension. In fact, because, as you will see, the IRS automatically grants a 30-day extension to anyone who asks, many experts recommend automatically asking for one each year, just in case. Speaking at an AP Now webinar, Greatland Corporation's Janice K. Krueger spelled out exactly what must be done in each situation in order to get the release.

Requesting the First Extension

Krueger pointed out that the IRS will grant an automatic 30-day filing extension, if the request is made. To do so, file Form 8809, *Application for Extension of Time to File Information Returns.*

Form 8809 must be filed by the due date of the return in order to be granted the extension. So, make sure you leave yourself plenty of time. In fact, if you automatically file this form each year, you'll be covered. File it in early January and then you don't have to worry.

The Form may 88-0 may be submitted on paper for one filer. However, it must be submitted through the FIRE (Filing Information Returns Electronically) system either as a fill-in form or an electronic file if requesting an extension for more than one filer.

Those requesting an extension for several types of forms you can do it in one of two ways. They can either

> – Complete a separate Form 8809 for each type of form, or

- Complete one Form 8809, but it must be submitted by the earliest due date for which an extension is being requested

Requesting Additional Extensions

Only the first extension is automatic. After that, you may submit one additional 30-day extension application. The additional extension is not automatically granted. The Form 8809 must be signed and an explanation must be included.

You will need to have a good reason for requesting the extension to have it granted. Krueger noted that only under extreme hardship conditions or catastrophic events is an additional 30-day extension granted.

She also noted that the automatic and any additional extension requests will only extend the due date for filing the returns. It does not extend the due date for furnishing statements to the recipients. They still must be sent on time.

Electronic Extension Request

The requests for extensions of time to file recipient copies for more than 10 payers are required to be submitted electronically. A signed letter must be faxed to the Information Returns Branch (IRB) by the transmitter the same day as the transmission. It must include reason an extension is needed. Krueger instructed attendees not to submit a list of payer names/TINs in this letter since this information is included in the electronic file.

Of course, the best approach to filing any IRS forms is to get them in before the due date. However, that is not always possible. Those who must file information returns late are advised to follow Krueger's fine advice for the best results.

You're Not Alone: Biggest 1099/W-9 Headaches

The game of bridge is played with two teams comprised of two players on each team. Sometimes, when a player feels his/her partner has made a particularly bad play, they'll joke that they have three opponents. We get the feeling that's how many accounts payable professionals feel when it comes to getting W-9s from their vendors. They not only have to battle with some vendors for this all-important document, they get pushback from within their own company, from the folks who are supposed to be on their side.

Single Biggest Problem

We recently asked our readers, as well as professionals in other groups, to identify the biggest problems they had when it came to the 1099 process. To be perfectly frank, we were a bit surprised at the issue that topped the list. What follows are the top five problems identified by survey respondents in the order of severity, with the top item being the biggest headache of them all.

- Pushback from purchasing and others on requiring W-9s
- Getting W-9s from all vendors
- Resolving Name/TIN Mismatches identified by IRS TIN Matching
- Getting approval to register to use IRS TIN Matching
- Management and others not understanding the 1099 issue

Biggest Problems Experiences by All

We then gave respondents the opportunity to identify all the problems they had regarding the 1099/W-9 issue and the results were somewhat different, as you can see from the list below.

- Getting W-9s from all vendor
- Handwritten W-9s that are difficult to read
- Vendors who refuse to return completed W-9s
- Management and others not understanding the 1099 issue
- Pushback from purchasing and others on requiring W-9s

To put this in perspective, over two-thirds of the respondents had trouble getting W-9s back from vendors while only about one-third reported pushback from purchasing and others on requiring W-9s. Still, that is a pretty hefty number and not one to be ignored.

Solution to the Pushback Issue

The main approach to the pushback issue, as well as management and others not understanding the whole 1099 situation is education. Of course, getting folks to listen when their plates are already overloaded is a difficult task, unless you have a high level finance or accounting exec, like the CFO on your side.

However, there is one technique that several reported using with great success. When the organization got hit with a big fine or penalty related to poor reporting, they used this red flag to get management's attention. By demonstrating actual losses (not potential or theoretical ones) these savvy professionals were finally able to get everyone to understand and follow the best practice of requiring a W-9 from every vendor. "We used the large B-Notice fines to convince the executives that the issue is important to the bottom line," explains one respondent. It is unfortunate that it had to come to that, but given the situation, it was a way to squeeze some lemonade out of the lemon of a fine.

Solutions to the Getting W-9 Problem

Is your reaction to the January 1099 process the same as one of our readers who says, "I pull my hair out and dread January." We believe this doesn't have to be, if you can garner some support for your approach from within your organization. The vendors in some ways are easier to deal with, again assuming you have that all-important management backing. What follows are tactics our survey respondents have used to deal with vendors who are reluctant to part with their tax information.

- Do not pay until the W-9 is received.
- We set up a policy that we would not pay a vendor without a completed W9
- We do not issue checks until a W-9 is received from the vendor. Money talks!
- A vendor is not input in the system until purchasing sends us a W-9 from the vendor. Usually they need to create a PO which can't be done until the vendor is created.
- We just refuse to enter a new vendor until we receive a W9.
- Invoices are not processed for payment until a completed W-9 has been received.

Do you notice a common theme in the tactics described above? These strategies only work if management supports the concept.

Not all the strategies used by our respondent were so stringent. We had two in particular that took a gentler approach. They are:

1) Have a cover sheet explaining to any vendors/contractors why your company needs a

1099, using the IRS requirements as your basis. Also save a PDF of a blank W-9 from the IRS's website on your computer so you can email your letter and the W-9 to new vendors/contractors.

2) Let anyone in a hiring position know they need to take care of the 1099 as part of hiring a contractor. If they would let you know ahead of time and you can provide them with the W-9 and cover letter.

Concluding Thoughts

I'm almost afraid to write this but let's throw caution to the wind. While the battles surrounding 1099s and getting W-9s are definitely ongoing, it appears that accounts payable is winning this one. The sheer number of respondents who indicated they were taking a strong stance on getting W-9s from vendors is in sharp contrast to just a few short years ago. Many are refusing to take No for an answer, and amazingly, they appear to be getting support from management.

Review Question – Chapter 5

1. When you cleanse the master vendor file which of the following should be part of the process?

> A. Purging inactive vendors
> B. Deactivating inactive vendors
> C. Updating contact info for inactive vendors
> D. Checking the Internet to see if the vendor is still in business

2. If you have trouble getting W-9s from vendors, which of the following will help alleviate that issue?

> A. Put your W-9 on your website
> B. Offer to give them your W-9
> C. Explain the reasoning to purchasing, hoping they'll explain to the supplier
> D. Don't pay until a W-9 is received

Explanations of the correct responses to the review questions are available at the end of the book starting on page 71.

Chapter 6:
The Finishing Touches

Eight Simple Ways to Make Year End Run Smoother

December and January do not have to be any more hectic than the rest of the year. Of course, for that to happen you have to take the appropriate steps to get ready before the year-end train comes hurling down the tracks once again wreaking havoc in its wake. Here are a few steps you can take to ensure a smoother year end.

1) Hire an intern to work over the holidays. If you have a few dollars left in your budget, hire a college student to help out over the holidays and perhaps in January while the student is on winter break. The student will appreciate the income and you will be able to get some of the more tedious work cleared out. In fact, if you post a notice on the company bulletin board, an employee in another department may have a child or niece or nephew that fits the bill. This is also a good way to try out a prospective employee.

2) Get travel & entertainment processing and reimbursements caught up. Few people travel towards the end of the year,

especially after December 15, so this is a good time to get T&E processing up to date. You might send reminders out to all travelers telling them to get their reimbursement requests in before December 10 (or whatever date appropriate for your organization) if they wish to be reimbursed before December 20 (or the appropriate date for your organization). Your goal is to make sure that you are not dealing with rush T&E requests on the last few days of the year when you are trying to get accounts payable's books closed.

3) Try to get all invoices into accounts payable as early in the month as possible. Then get them all entered into the system. If you have a backlog, the intern discussed in step one will help. This will help with your accrual process as well as improve the accuracy of those accruals.

4) Don't leave year end reviews until the end of December. You know when they are coming, so get them started in November—at least how the raise and promotion budget will be allocated along with all the paper work. Whether you tell your employees or not will depend on company policy.

5) December is a terrible time for rush checks. Send a notice saying that no rush

checks will be issued and all invoices need to be delivered to accounts payable before December 20 (or the appropriate date for your group). Do not expect to be 100% successful with this initiative but if you can reduce the number of invoices arriving on the 30th and 31st, you will have made the close a little smoother.

6) Stop wasting time in December trying to track down the social security numbers of the independent contractors used during the year. If you do not already have a policy of requiring a W-9 from every vendor before you do business with them, institute it now. It puts an end to the December/January madness that sometimes accompanies the issuance of 1099.

7) Stop wasting time in October and November trying to reconcile discrepancies reported by the IRS on B-Notices, those awful notices the IRS sends to let you know the information you filed earlier in the year was not correct. Mismatches between the name and the taxpayer identification number are frequent. Reduce your mismatches to almost nothing by participating in the IRS TIN Matching program and using it throughout the year.

8) Make approving invoices for payment and returning them to accounts payable for processing a top priority. This will make AP run smoother with fewer vendor inquiries, improve vendor relations and reduce duplicate payments, making your organization more profitable.

None of the strategies recommended here is earth shattering; all are within the realm of everyone reading this. By implementing them you will improve the efficiency of the accounting department and perhaps have employees who are a little less harried.

The Last Detail: Thanking the Staff

When all the tasks associated with the close are finally complete and memories of 1099 nightmares fading fast, there's one more task to be completed; and it's often overlooked. Don't forget to thank the staff for all their extra efforts. This is finally the time to focus on improving the way the staff feels about its work. Even accounts payable departments where the mood is generally good can stand an occasional surprise or morale booster. Here are three tactics any organization can use to raise staff spirits after the close.

1) Have a high level executive from your organization thank the staff for their hard efforts. This can be done in the form of a surprise visit to the department or by sending individual letters to

each employee.

2) After the staff has put in extra efforts to get year-end closed, send everyone home early one Friday afternoon. Alternatively, they can be released early on the day before a holiday, say Presidents' Day. For this to be truly effective, it needs to be on a day when other departments are not leaving early. If coverage is an issue, send half the staff home one Friday and the rest the following week.

3) Surprise the staff one afternoon by bringing in an ice cream treat. Depending on your office setup, it can be individual pops or a more elaborate make-your-own Sundae affair.

These are just simple examples of what you can do with a little ingenuity and even less money. You can probably come up with even better ways to let your staff know they are appreciated.

None of the suggestions provided cost a lot of money; in fact two of them will make no impact whatsoever on the bottom line. The important feature is they show the staff they are appreciated and someone is thinking about them. While money's nice, thoughtfulness can have an even bigger impact on morale and team spirits. And, that's the whole purpose of this exercise.

Next Year Will Be Different: Laying the Groundwork for a Better Close Next Year

You've finally finished dealing with the year-end

close. Every last task has been completed. You're ready to move on to your next project and forget about the hassles and nightmares of the last few weeks. If your close has run anything other than picture-perfect smoothly, resist that temptation. For if you take a little extra time right now, next year truly should be a little less of a battle. What follows is a game plan for a smoother close next year.

The Game Plan

Step 1. Keep notes throughout the close noting everything that goes especially well. Regrettably, this may be a short list. If you can pinpoint the reason, make sure you include it. These notes do not have to be detailed but they should include enough commentary so you will know what action to take at a later date.

Step 2. Keep notes throughout the close of every situation where there was a problem. Note also the people and/or departments who were involved. This is not so there can be finger pointing at a later date, but so you know who you will need to deal with on the issue.

Step 3. Ask the people on your staff who do the lion's share of the work related to the close to do the same. Don't allow people to wait until after the close is complete because much of the important detail will be forgotten. In fact, to make sure everyone is keeping notes, you might ask that they submit them at the end of each week. This will force people to focus on their commentary.

Step 4. Gather all the notes and prioritize the problems as you see them, with the goal of working on alleviating the top items first. Be careful in how you prioritize for if there are more than a few issues on your list, the odds are high that you won't have time to work on them all before the next year end.

Step 5. Cross off any items on the list that you know are not likely to be resolved. This can be both for political reasons as well as operational reasons.

Step 6. Consider having a staff meeting, perhaps a luncheon to than the team for their hard work, and review the list. Get their input. They may offer simple solutions to some of the problems. Or they may have different insights as to what caused the problems and/or how they can be fixed.

Step 7. Revise your priorities and start working on fixing the issues that caused your yearend problems.

Step 8. Take the list of problems with easy solutions and work on them as well, even if the items are lower on the priority list. This will give the group some easy wins and eliminate some headaches without a ton of work.

Concluding Thoughts

The process described above is not a one-shot deal. It should be followed every year, for like it or not, new problems will emerge as time goes on. Follow the plan and with a little luck, next year will be different—and in a good way!

Review Questions – Chapter 6

1. When is the best time to collect the social security numbers of the independent contractors you do business with?

    A. You don't need to collect them
    B. When you begin the relations, before you pay them
    C. In December, it's easier if you collect them all at once
    D. Whenever the staff has some free time

2. Once all the problems from the current year are resolved, which of the following should be your course of action during the next fiscal close?

    A. You can let the staff off the hook as far as keeping their eyes opened for problems as you've fixed everything and you'll notice any problems yourself
    B. You can avoid the annoying note taking about problems because you've fixed all the problems
    C. Assign one staffer to keep their eyes open for problems and let everyone else stop with the notes
    D. Both the manager and staff should keep notes again regarding any new problems that may have crept in.

Explanations of the correct responses to the review questions is available at the end of the book

Glossary of Terms

Accrual - a charge incurred in one accounting
period that will be paid for in a later period

ACH – Automated Clearing House

ACH credit – An electronic payment initiated by
the payor

B-Notice - An annual IRS notification to payers,
that IRS Forms 1099 have been filed with either
missing or incorrect name/TIN combinations.

Duplicate Payment – The unintentional second
payment of an invoice. One type of erroneous
payment and unfortunately, rarely returned by
the vendor unless the customer or its audit firm
discover the over payment.

e-Invoice – An electronic invoice either provided
through an automated approach or as simple
attachment to an e-mail. Some do not consider
files attached to e-mail as true electronic
invoices.

Form 1099 – The Form 1099 is used to report
different types of taxable income; the most
common for the accounts payable groups being
Form 1099MISC. This is used to report income
paid to independent contractors.

IFO – Institute of Financial Operations

Internal Controls - The group of policies and procedures implemented within the organization to prevent intentional or unintentional misuse of funds for unauthorized purposes.

NACHA - National Automated Clearing House Association

Packing slip – Sometimes referred to as receiving documents, delineates exactly what was delivered in a particular shipment. Used in the three-way match.

PO – Purchase Order

Receiving documents – See packing slip.

S-Ox – Sarbanes Oxley Act

Segregation of Duties – With regards to accounts payable, it is the division of work so that one person does not perform more than one leg of the procure-to-pay function. It is one of the foundation principles of strong internal controls.

Three-way Match – Comparison of invoice with purchase order and receiving documents before payment is made. If there is a discrepancy, some investigation is required to eliminate the discrepancy before payment is made.

T&E – Travel and Entertainment

W-9 – Its full name is Request for Taxpayer Identification Number and Certification and it is provided to customers who need to verify certain tax reporting information.

Index

1

1099 · iii, 46, 48, 51, 52, 53, 55, 59, 60, 66

A

accrual · 9, 42, 43, 44, 58
ACH · 66
Annual performance reviews · 6
ASAP check · *See* Rush Check
Automated Clearing House · *See* ACH

B

B-Notice · 53, 66
budget · 6, 12, 57, 58
Budget · 6, 12

C

calendar · 5, 10, 39, 40, 41

E

e-Invoice · *See* electronic invoice
electronic invoice · 66
escheat · 59
Excel · 40
Expense Reimbursements · iii, 30
expense reports · 30, 31, 32, 33, 35, 38, 44

F

Form 8809 · 49, 50

I

intern · 57, 58
internal controls · 67
IRS · 6, 46, 47, 48, 49, 51, 52, 55, 59, 66

L

laggard · 34
last call · 8, 9

M

Morale · 11

N

Next Close · 40

O

open credits · 8

P

PO · 47, 54, 67
purchase order · 67

R

reimbursement · 9, 31, 33, 34, 58

S

schedule · 6, 7, 11, 39, 41, 47

T

T&E · 30, 31, 32, 34, 35, 36, 58, 67
TIN information · 47
TIN Matching · 46, 47, 48, 52, 60

W

W-9 · 47, 51, 52, 53, 54, 55, 56, 59, 67

Review Questions Explained

Review Questions Chapter 1

1) To get ready for year-end, which of the following tasks should be completed?

- A. **Correct.** If you print your own 1099s, ordering the forms early will ensure you can get the 1099s issued on time. It will also remove some of the stress inevitably associated with year-end.
- B. Incorrect. While allowing employees to take vacation time over year-end might improve morale for the employee involved, it will make the year-end close more difficult for those who do not take vacation.
- C. Incorrect. Ignoring disputed invoices will create problems later on and as much as possible should be cleared up before year end.
- D. Incorrect. While it might be nice of begin planning for new projects for next year, there is too much other work associated with a smooth close that should take priority.

2) With regards to un-cashed checks that have been outstanding for a long time, which action should be taken at year-end?

- A. Incorrect. Writing un-cashed checks off to miscellaneous income is a sure-fire way to have unclaimed property auditors insist on the funds being turned over to the states for escheat purposes.

B. **Correct.** Following up on un-cashed checks is required by the states as part of escheat due diligence. As an added bonus it helps companies determine if these items can be reversed.

C. Incorrect. Un-cashed checks are legal obligations of the organization and should not be voided – unless a new check is written.

D. Incorrect. Unfortunately, un-cashed checks, if ignored are, likely to remain on the books forever. Rarely will they will be cashed

Review Questions – Chapter 2

1. At year-end, to ensure a smooth a close as possible, who should be sent special notices to remind them of deadlines?

A.   Incorrect. Sending reminders to all vice presidents will not improve the close with regards to invoices or expense reports that should have been submitted.

B.   **Correct.** By sending reminders to known laggards, there is an increased chance they will send in the invoices or expense reports they "forgot" to send in earlier.

C.   Incorrect. Sending a special notice to the purchasing manager will only help if he/she is typically late. It will not help with others who are also late.

D.   Incorrect. While the sales manager may or may not be tardy with his/her expense report, they rarely have invoices to be submitted so sending them a special notice will have limited value.

2. What is the best way to reduce the number of discrepant invoices?

A.   Incorrect. Refusing to handle discrepant invoices throwing the problem back to the vendor is likely to incense vendors and consequently not help the issue or vendor relations.

B.   Incorrect. Accounts payable is not a position to decide who the company will do business with and how they won't. What's more an organization often can't stop doing business with those vendors who have the most discrepancies, as they are often critical vendors.

C.   Incorrect. Ignoring all discrepancies and paying what you think is correct will result in a nightmare situation with vendors and is a poor practice.

D.   **Correct.** By identifying common root causes for discrepant invoices and working to eliminate them will result not only in a smoother close, but a smoother invoice processing operation year round. Be aware, however, that there will always be discrepant invoices. All you can do is work to minimize them.

3. Vendor statements should be requested and reviewed how frequently?

A. Incorrect. If you never request supplier statements, many open credits will never be recouped as suppliers almost never automatically write checks for open credits.

B.**Correct.** If statements are requested and review at least once a year, if not more frequently, there is a good chance most of the open credits available will be identified and hopefully recouped.

C.Incorrect. If an organization only requests statements only every two or three years, many credits will be lost as vendors use them for items their customers would not agree with.

D. Incorrect. Requesting statements on a daily basis would create great vendor dissatisfaction and no vendor would comply.

Review Questions – Chapter 3

1.   What is the main reason some employees turn in their expense reports late?

- A. **Correct.** Unfortunately, as in other things in life, when it comes to expense reports some employees push the envelope. And, when their companies allow them to do so, despite written policies, (by paying their expenses) they continue with this poor behavior.
- B. Incorrect. Most employees have too much work; it is not an excuse to shirk the expense reporting obligations.
- C. Incorrect. This is absolutely false; most organizations what their employees to turn in their expense reports on time.
- D. Incorrect. Companies do not encourage employees to turn in their expense reports late; they do just the opposite.

2. Which of the following tactics will encourage employees to turn their expense reports on time?

- A. **Correct.** By refusing to pay all late fees for employees, companies put the penalty for late reporting squarely where it belongs: with the employee. Forced to pay late fees themselves, most employees will find the time to do their expense reports.
- B. Incorrect. Making credit card payments for employees, even if expense reports

have not been received just encourages employees in their behavior. It's positive reinforcement for bad behavior.

C. Incorrect. Giving cash advances makes it difficult for some employees to hand their expense reports in on time. If there is excess cash advance to be returned, many will drag their feet with their reporting.

D. Incorrect. Reminding employees and their supervisors of late expense reports helps get reports turned in on time. So, if you skip this step, the reverse is likely to happen.

Review Questions – Chapter 4

1. Why is it important to keep notes on problems encountered during the close?

A. Incorrect. GAAP makes no specific mention of keeping notes during the close.
B. Incorrect. Apportioning blame in any situation is not a way to build a team, encourage cooperation or improve morale. It should be avoided unless it is a last resort.
C. **Correct.** By planning on how to avoid problems next year, you take a giant step towards a smoother close. Notes will help you with that.
D. Incorrect. Getting another department to take on the tasks you have problems with is not a good idea. If it belongs in your department, figure out how to do it right.

2. Why are accruals so important?

A. Incorrect. Accruals are not used for tax purposes.
B. Incorrect. There is no basis in the law for doing accruals.
C. Incorrect. Accruals have no impact on staffing.
D. **Correct.** Accruals help give an accurate financial picture of the organization by correctly providing expenses and income for

the period. This can then be used for planning purposes.

Review Question – Chapter 5

1. When you cleanse the master vendor file which of the following should be part of the process?

A. Incorrect. Purging inactive vendors will result in losing information that could be needed at a later date.

B. **Correct.** Deactivating inactive vendors is the best approach as it prevents someone from using the entry in the master vendor file while preserving the data, should it be needed at a later date. This could occur if a vendor claimed it hadn't been paid.

C. Incorrect. There is absolutely no reason to update contact info for inactive vendors. It's a waste of time.

D. Incorrect. Checking the Internet to see if the vendor is still in business will have little value if you are not doing any business with them.

2. If you have trouble getting W-9s from vendors, which of the following will help alleviate that issue?

A. Incorrect. Putting your W-9 on your website will help companies your organization might sell to but will have no impact on your vendors.

B. Incorrect. Offering to give vendors your

W-9 is worthless as they have no need for your information.

C. Incorrect. Explaining the reasoning to purchasing, hoping they'll explain to the supplier is not a good use of your time as they will rarely do as you want.

D. **Correct.** By not paying until a W-9 is received, you are in the best position to get the W-9. This is the time when you have the leverage, so make the most of it.

Review Questions – Chapter 6

1. When is the best time to collect the social security numbers of the independent contractors you do business with?

- A. Incorrect. You absolutely do need to collect social security numbers from your independent contractors so you can issue 1099s to them in January.
- B. **Correct.** When you begin the relations, before you pay them is when you hold the most leverage. So, make the most of it and don't pay until the social security information you need is provided.
- C. Incorrect. It is not easier to collect all social security number information at one time. That is a nightmare and independent contractors with whom you are no longer doing business are likely not to provide the data.
- D. Incorrect. If you wait until the staff has some free time, you'll wait forever and never get the social security numbers you need to issue 1099s in January.

2. Once all the problems from the current year are resolved, which of the following should be your course of action during the next fiscal close?

A. Incorrect. Your staff sees problems you as a manger don't. Letting them off the hook as far as keeping their eyes opened for problems means you'll miss some of the problems when they first start.

B. Incorrect. While you may have fixed all the problems, this doesn't mean new ones won't pop up. So, you can't let your guard down.

C. Incorrect. By assigning only one staffer to keep their eyes open for problems, you are limiting the chances of finding all problems before they turn into major-league nightmares.

D. **Correct.** If both the manager and staff keep notes again regarding any new problems that may have crept in, your organization is in the very best position to nip problems in the bud. This should keep year end running smoothly as small problems will be fixed before they turn into big ones.

MARY S. SCHAEFFER

Excerpt:
101 Best Practices for
Accounts Payable

Excerpt

The Issue: Handling Unidentified Invoices

More often that you'd think, an invoice shows up in the accounts payable department with no identification as to who ordered the product. Occasionally these invoices will float from desk to desk throughout the company before finding their way into accounts payable. Sometimes by looking at what is included on the invoice, a savvy accounts payable associate will be able to figure out who the likely purchaser is and will then forward the invoice to that person for approval.

However, that is frequently not the case, especially in the case of generic goods like printer cartridges or paper for the copy machine. Often the dollar amount involved is small and does not appear to be worth the time and effort to research who ordered the goods. These are especially problematic as there is a higher incidence of fraud with these invoices than might be expected.

Best Practice: The best approach is to send these unidentified invoices back to the sender asking them to indicate who ordered the goods. To be clear, an unidentified invoice is one that does not have either a purchase order number or name of a requisitioner. Include a polite letter stating that it is your organization's policy to require this information so you may get the invoice paid as quickly as possible. By showing the vendor how they will benefit by including this information, they will be more likely to adapt to your requirements. By the way, this requirement, as well as any other accounts payable requirement, should be included in your terms and conditions provided to the vendor at the beginning of the relationship. This stance is especially important in the case of small dollar items. (See Worst Practices below).

Almost Best Practice: If it is not feasible to simply return the invoice, pick up the phone and call the vendor. When provided with the information, request that in the future the vendor include the requestors' names on invoices. If this is a recurring problem, keep a list of vendors who routinely omit the purchasers' name along with the employees' names who regularly order from these companies. Again, ask the employees to request that their name or department be included on all invoices.

Special Pointers for Accounts Payable: This is one of those headaches that in all likelihood will never go away completely. However, accounts payable can and should do what it can to minimize the problem. By working with these suppliers, many of whom are small and will be amenable to listening to suggestions (rather than demands); accounts payable will be able to make a dent in the problem.

Worst Practice: Simply paying for the goods reasoning that the dollar amount is too small to

.

bother with. This can quickly get your company on the sucker list. More than a few companies out there prey upon overworked accounts payable departments. They send along invoices for goods not ordered, knowing full well that small dollar invoices are often paid without authorization. Once you pay that unidentified invoice once, your company will be hit over and over again – and probably for increasingly larger amounts of money as time goes on.

Excerpt: Accounts Payable Now & Tomorrow newsletter

EACH ISSUE CONTAINS 4-6 ARTICLES, A BEST PRACTICE DIAGNOSTIC QUIZ, A SHORT ON NEW TERMINOLOGY, ONE PAGE OF REGULATORY UPDATES AND TWO PAGES OF SHORT TIPS.

WHAT FOLLOWS IS THE MATERIAL FROM A RECENT ISSUE

Emerging Payment Issues
Combatting ACH Fraud

Electronic payment fraud, frequently called ACH fraud, involves a third-party fraudulently accessing funds they have no right via the ACH. Too often, organizations think they do not have to be concerned about this type of fraud because they don't make electronic payments themselves. Unfortunately, nothing could be further from the truth. Everyone is at risk. Recognizing this growing risk, AP Now's editorial director, Mary Schaeffer and Claudia Swendseid, a senior vice president from the Federal Reserve Bank of Minneapolis teamed up at the IFO's Fusion conference, to make a presentation on how to combat this deadly threat.

How Serious Is The Problem?

According to statistics from the Association of Financial Professionals (AFP), one out of every five businesses experienced an actual or attempted ACH fraud last year. What is really great about the AFP data is that they not only report on successful frauds, they also share statistics on frauds that were successfully thwarted.

So, how successful were companies at making sure the crooks who tried to perpetrate a fraud using the ACH didn't succeed? Only 17% of the businesses with ACH fraud attempts against them, actually suffered a loss.

Looking at it from another perspective, Bank Credit, Price & Customer Service Treasury Management Monitor Report to Respondents, by Phoenix-Hecht for 2012, reports that one in ten companies that experienced major fraud issue said the fraud involved ACH.

What these numbers demonstrate is that ACH fraud is a serious concern and one that all organizations need to take seriously. Just a few short years ago, this type of deceit was not even on our horizon.

How ACH Fraud Happens

One of the most frightening features of ACH fraud is the proliferation of approaches that can be used to perpetrate this crime. Crooks operating in this arena are quite knowledgeable about the banking system and the use of technology. They marry to two to create unique approaches to their craft. We don't think we've seen the end of their creativity. AT this point their approaches boil down to the following four broad categories:

1) **Unauthorized debits to accounts**. This approach began with the positive pay rejects from the paper check world being represented as ACH debits. You can imagine how upset companies were who thought they'd purchased the best payment fraud protection. While positive pay is the best defense against check fraud, that's all it protects against. It does nothing to

help with other types of payment fraud, such as ACH. Other techniques used include use of unauthorized debits as well as invalid or counterfeit ACH debits

2) **Insider origination fraud**. This is exactly what it sounds like; one of your employees falsifying transactions for personal gain. It is the newest type of occupational fraud.

3) **Reverse phishing**. Typically, this involves the sending of e-mails that look legitimate. Their purpose is to either collect information they have no right to (such as your bank account numbers) for use in perpetrating their frauds or to entice you to make a change, usually to a vendor's Remit-To bank account number, which is fraudulent.

4) **Corporate account takeovers**. This particularly insidious fraud involves the taking over the vendor's bank account for the purpose of issuing of fraudulent ACH payments. Typically it involves the downloading of malware on an employee's to collect keystrokes, which provide the thief with the needed account information and passwords to "take over the account" and create ACH credits to parties of the fraudster's choosing.

Protection against ACH Debit Fraud

As most readers are aware, ACH debit activity is initiated by the payee, not the payor. To prevent frauds the rely on ACH debits, take the following steps:

- Limit ACH debit activity to one or two bank accounts. This limits your potential exposure.

- Reconcile your bank accounts daily and notify your bank of any suspicious transactions. By doing this you should be able to recover all unauthorized transactions. If you wait longer, all the money may not be recoverable. Organizations have a 24-hour window of opportunity, in this regard. After that, they are not guaranteed the return of their funds, although their banks will do their best to recover all funds taken fraudulently.

- Make sure your staff addresses exceptions in a timely manner

- Use fraud prevention services offered by your bank. Make sure you read the description of the product offered to ensure you understand what protection is being offered. There is little uniformity among the products offered by different banks, so don't assume you know what each does, simply by reading its name. Products currently offered include:

- ACH blocks on all accounts where ACH debit activity will not be used

- ACH filters

- ACH positive pay or if available, payee name positive pay

- ACH debit alerts that notify you when ACH debits arrive, if your bank offers them

- Secure your bank account information; lock up paper documents and limit access to sensitive online data. Don't underestimate the value of this step. Crooks have been known to go dumpster diving in corporate dumpsters to look for critical information – like your bank account numbers.

Protection against ACH Credit Fraud

Too often when companies think about ACH fraud protection, they only consider ACH debit fraud. But, ACH credit fraud can be even more devastating because it usually involves the takeover of the bank account. Here are some of the steps you can take to protect your organization's bank accounts:

- Implement best practices for online and IT data security, including

- Adopting a stronger form of authentication or added layers of security

- Dedicating a separate PC for payments origination and do NOT use it for anything else, especially e-mail and surfing the Internet

- Use dual controls for payment origination and account set-up. In this manner, even if one computer is corrupted and taken over, the crook will only have half the information they need to take over the bank account.

    - Implement proactive detection and monitoring. Regularly check with your bank about new products being offered

Protection against All Types of Fraud

Don't forget to educate all employees on fraud and fraud prevention techniques. Sometimes the training is reserved for managers and other senior level employees. But that is not adequate. This is information that everyone needs, if the organization is to be adequately protected.

Also as mentioned earlier, the crooks in this arena, unfortunately, are not stupid. They know how the banking system works and they have a good understanding of how fraud protection products and procedures work. So, whenever the banking and business community develop a way to prevent a particular approach, the fraudsters go back to the drawing board and come up with a new technique.

Therefore it is critical that every professional keep updated on the newest frauds being perpetrated so they can watch for them and make sure their organization isn't adversely affected by these frauds. This also means regularly talking with your banks to discover what they are doing to stop these frauds and what new products are available.

Fraud prevention and detection is a never-ending process. You can't let your guard down for one minute. For if you do, some crafty thief will find a way to take advantage.

Internal Control Questions from the Trenches

When it comes to internal controls, there's no limit to the areas touched. Our editorial director found that out recently when she gave two talks on the Breakdown of Internal Controls in the accounts payable process. What follows are a small portion of the questions (with the responses) she was asked.

Q: Why not issue a check instead of an ACH

payment; doesn't the check leave a better paper trail?

A: While paper checks leave paper trails, that is all they leave. And for it to do you any good, someone has to dig through old checks. Checks are much more risky. They can be stolen in the mail; un-cashed they have unclaimed property reporting and remitting requirements and they are expensive to produce (postage and man-hours). Electronic payments leave an electronic trail that can be easily accessed by all interested parties.

Q: Who would be in the best position to ensure leaving employees turn their cards in and have their accesses rescinded?

A: If the employee is leaving the organization, the exit interview should not only include retrieving the key to the building but also any company credit cards. This task usually falls to HR and the tasks related to accounts payable frequently fall through the cracks. That's why it is so important for AP or the card administrator to be notified so they can cancel the card with the bank. Then, even if the employee tries to use it, it won't go through.

Q: For travel expenses, what do you think about allowances versus payments based on receipts?

A: I think you are talking about per-diems. I like them because they eliminate a lot of the headaches associated with T&E. If you were a US company, I'd warn you of making sure they conformed to GSA guidelines or you could have IRS problems. You may have similar restrictions in Canada. Be forewarned, that this is an issue you can never win with. If you go to a per-diem approach, your modest spenders will be thrilled while your lavish spenders will complain bitterly.

Q: What is the percentage of organizations having T&E fraud?

A: In its 2012 Report to the Nation, The ACFE reports that 14.5% of all respondents to its survey had expense reimbursement fraud.

Q. A lot of credit card companies usually contain incentives to encourage new members to sign up (frequent traveler/spending points). Although not a direct expense to the company, what type of controls could be put in place to prevent this? Or is this not really a concern?

A: If the company has a corporate card that it arranges, it can completely control this issue. If employees put charges on their personal cards, then the card the employee choses is left to his or her discretion. Be aware, they could be tempted to purchase airlines at higher rates to earn more points, if there are cash rebates based on spend. It's one of the many reasons, a corporate card is recommended.

Q. What are the potential risks of duplicate

vendors in the vendor master files?

A: This all depends on whether or not best practices related to the master vendor file are used and if so, whether they are all used or just some. The fewer best practices used, the more likely there will be duplicate vendors in the master vendor file.

Q. How often should we perform a Payment Audit?

A: Aside from the obvious recovery of funds, one of the benefits of a payment audit is it helps identify weaknesses that may have crept into your process. The sooner these are identified and fixed, the better off you will be. Therefore, it is recommended that a payment audit be performed at least annually, if not more frequently. It is also recommended that you try and collect as much of the low-hanging fruit as you can before calling in the pros.

Q. Who should have access to Vendor Master File?

A: It depends on the reason for the access. Anyone who has a business need to see the information should have access. However, when it comes to adding new vendors or updating information, that access should be limited to the few people responsible for the master vendor file. Of course, those people should not be working on any other leg of the procure-to-pay process.

Q. How can a small firm with only a few employees working in accounts payable have the appropriate controls while maintaining appropriate segregation of duties?

A: This is an excellent question and one we anticipate being asked more frequently as organizations automate the invoice processing function. It is inevitable that when that happens, accounts payable departments will shrink in size. The first step smaller accounts payable departments take is to look for functions that can effectively be moved to another department. Typically, that includes responsibility for the master vendor file and/or signing of checks—if the appropriate segregation of duties can still be maintained. Once everything that can be moved has been, if there are still internal control issues, institute some checks and balances into the process. Yes, this means more work. But given, the limited number of other alternatives, it is your only option.

Paperless AP for Companies without a Budget to Get Rid of the Paper

If you are like most people affiliated with the accounts payable function, you'd probably do almost anything to get rid of the mountains of paper. If you are lucky, you work for a company that actually has budget to do just that *and* has spent it on that process. Alas, many of the rest of us can only dream of such an existence. But this does not have to be. Lack of budget does not mean you have to completely forgo the benefits of an electronic accounts payable department. Let's take a look at seven strategies any organization can use to get rid of some of the paper—and they don't cost a red cent.

1) Start accepting invoices electronically. Typically, e-mailed invoices arrive in the form of a PDF attachment. If you print the attachment, you're not getting rid of much paper. So, figure out how you want to store these documents in a centralized location. Some retraining of processors might also be called for as they learn how to deal with an electronic document instead of a paper one.

2) Have faxed invoices sent to an e-fax facility. This will automatically convert faxes to e-mails and you'll never have to deal with the paper. Once you have this in placed, your so-called faxed invoices can be treated exactly like e-mailed invoices.

3) Make payments to vendors electronically. This will help get rid of those awful paper checks. And, not only will you get rid of some of the paper, electronic payments are cheaper than paper checks.

4) Send remittance advices to vendors for e-payments via e-mail. This simple step will make a huge difference in whether or not some vendors

accept payments electronically. By providing this information directly to the person handling cash applications, the problems many vendors have with electronic payments disappear. And, again, there's no paper.

5) Send an e-mail with explanations of short payments to vendors, if information doesn't fit on remittance advice. The beauty of this approach is by taking the initiative you not only improve vendor relationships; you also reduce the number of calls coming into accounts payable.

6) Automate your expense reporting process even if it's only e-mailing an Excel version of your expense reports for approval and then for reimbursement. Of course, if using Excel remember to lock the formulas to prevent employees from trying to play games with reimbursement requests.

7) Make electronic payments (ACH) mandatory for all expense reimbursements. While many states still will not allow you to mandate electronic payments for payroll, you can do so for expense reimbursements.

As you can see, none of the strategies proposed are difficult or require budget. They may necessitate a change in process, but that is easily managed. And once you've made these changes, don't forget to update your policy and procedures manual as well as train all affected employees.

5 Simple and Quick Ways to Improve Accounts Payable Productivity

There are so many productivity zappers in accounts payable, it's hard to know where to start when asked to identify some or all of them. What follow are five steps any department can take to make the accounts payable function just a little more productive.

Tactic #1: Minimize the number of duplicate invoices being sent to accounts payable. While many vendors are willing to e-mail invoices, more than a few of them are also mailing them at the same time. They want to "make sure" their invoices are received. They give no thought to the extra work this entails at the other end. Identify those vendors who are sending both paper and e-mailed invoices and request that they stop. Sometimes this is all it takes, but not always.

Once you've weeded out those who you can get to stop, develop an Always Check Thoroughly (ACT) list for those who refuse to stop. Closely monitor those accounts to ensure you don't pay them twice. Some companies have taken the step of actually discarding the paper invoices received from these companies, not even bothering to open their envelopes.

Tactic #2: Get rid of as many paper checks as possible. They are inefficient and problematic and drain resources the accounts payable function could be using elsewhere on more value-add tasks. Instead, they are deployed handling the various transactional tasks associated with issuing paper checks. By moving some of the payments to a corporate procurement program and others to an electronic payment (ACH) program, much of the resources allocated to manual tasks associated with paper checks can be redeployed elsewhere.

Tactic #3: Spend as little time as possible dealing with duplicate payments. Of course to do this, you have to make very few, if any duplicate payments. Inexplicably, that is not as difficult as you might think, at first glance. Establish rigid coding standards for data entry and processing routines used by everyone handling invoices. This will go a long way towards eliminating duplicate payments.

To be effective in this regards, managers must eliminate creativity when it comes to processing invoices. If someone has an idea on how to do the process more effectively, they can simply bring it to the manger for review. If it's a good idea, then it can be implemented department wide.

Tactic #4: Don't waste time trying to figure out who should approve an unidentified invoice. By an unidentified invoice, we simply mean one that includes no information as to who ordered the goods or services. Every invoice, at a minimum, should have either the name of the purchaser and/or a purchase order number. Without this minimum amount of information it is difficult to find the correct person to approve the payment.

Rather than waste valuable accounts payable resources on this task, simply return it to the vendor with a polite letter requesting this missing information. It can be couched in terms of needing the information to get the vendor paid as quickly as possible.

Tactic #5: Keep paper checks out of the expense reimbursement process. Insist that all travel and entertainment expense reimbursements be done electronically with ACH. Don't issue paper checks. They are expensive, time consuming, problematic and make the process inefficient.

Have you taken all these steps already? If not, what are you waiting for?

An Efficient Process for Handling Invoices Sent by e-Mail

Trying to stop vendors from sending invoices by e-mail is like trying to stop the water once the dam or levy has broken. Given the inevitability of e-mailed invoices, it is far better to develop an effective plan to take advantage of this new delivery method than to fight it. What follows is a rather simple seven-step process any organization can use to address the receipt of e-mailed invoices situation.

Step 1: Recognize that you can't fight the proverbial City Hall and establish a formal policy for handling e-mailed invoices. This should be part of your formal policy and procedures manual for the accounts payable function.

Step 2: Set up one e-mail address to receive invoices from suppliers. This should be part of your best practice strategy to receive all e-mails in one centralized location. Today that means one postal address, one e-mail address and one fax address. The e-mail address should not a personal address but one that can be accessed by several people. This way, if someone is unexpectedly out of the office or leaves the company, there is no disruption to vendors e-mailing invoices.

Step 3: Provide the email address established for the receipt of invoices to all suppliers. This can be done in both the Welcome Packet for new vendors and the annual letter to vendors. If you normally don't send an annual letter to vendors, you might send a special communication regarding this e-mail address.

Step 4: Vendors should be informed that only invoices should be sent to this address. Nothing else sent to that address will be forwarded to other parties.

Step 5: Vendors should be instructed not to send

a second invoice by snail mail. Be aware that some will disregard this directive. Watch this process and create a list of vendors who always double submit despite your instructions. Paper invoices from these vendors should be discarded.

Step 6: Different people should be assigned to monitor the account on different days. They can also fill in for each other when someone is out or on vacations.

Step 7: Upon receipt of an invoice, it should immediately be reviewed and forwarded to the appropriate party for approval.

Typically, e-mailed invoices are first turned into a PDF and then sent to the customer. Great care needs to be taken that each is only processed once. For if you print the PDF, the hundredth printing will look just as good as the first one and you won't be able to tell which is the original and which is the copy. This means that routines for weeding out duplicates are more important than ever. It should also entail duplicate payment checking routines be integrated into the invoice processing function.

Invoices that are e-mailed are a reality every organization has to deal with. Trying to avoid the issue is not smart. Following a game plan, such as the one discussed above, is your best strategy for making this new approach work for your organization.

Best Practice Checklist: Departing Employees: Have You Covered All the Bases?

Whether an employee leaves the company for a big new fancy job or was invited to leave by the organization, there's a lot to be done. And unfortunately, a lot of it falls through the cracks. Do you think you catch all the details? Use our Departing Employee Checklist below to see if you've done everything you should, including the special ones related to accounts payable. After you've marked the checklist, see the best practice discussion of the responses that follows.

1. Do you retrieve all credit cards (T&E, p-card, fuel, one card) before the employee leaves? ____ Yes ____ No
2. Do you immediately notify the card issuing bank to cancel the credit cards? ____ Yes ____ No
3. Do you immediately notify the bank to cancel any signing authorizations of departing employees for either paper checks or electronic payments? ____ Yes ____ No
4. Do you retrieve the key to the building, if employees have them? ____ Yes ____ No
5. Do you retrieve all ID badges? ____ Yes ____ No

6. Do you immediately cut off system access, including windows login on desktops?
____ Yes ____ No

7. Do you deactivate the employee in the master vendor file if they are included for expense reimbursement purposes?
____ Yes ____ No

8. Do you request all outstanding expense reports, as soon as you know the employee is leaving? ____ Yes ____ No

9. Do you request repayment of all outstanding travel advances, if your organization gives them? ____ Yes ____ No

10. Do you cancel all subscriptions (both print and online) requesting a refund for the unused amount? ____ Yes ____ No

11. Do you cancel all subscriptions to specialized databases requesting a refund for unused amounts? (Note: Some simply transfer these to the employee taking on the departing employee's responsibilities)
____ Yes ____ No

12. Do you address the issue of the telephone line, either returning the number to the phone company or turning it over to someone else to handle any incoming calls? ____ Yes ____ No

13. Is the employee's email accounts terminated or assigned to be read by someone else? ____ Yes ____ No

14. If the e-mail account is assigned to someone else, is the password changed?
____ Yes ____ No

15. Is the employee's voice mail account terminated or assigned to be handled by someone else? ___ Yes ___ No

16. If the voice mail account is assigned to someone else, is the password changed? ___ Yes ___ No

17. Do you make sure you have a complete list of what employee is doing? (Note: Often employees perform tasks that are not included in the policy and procedures manual.) ___ Yes ___ No

18. Do you retrieve any laptop or cell phone or other equipment owned by the company but used by the employee? ___ Yes ___ No

19. Do you retrieve any other company belongings such as manuals etc.? ___ Yes ___ No

20. Do you make sure you have a current forwarding address for the employee? ___ Yes ___ No

21. If the employee is an authorized purchaser, do you contact suppliers and vendors to remove employee as authorized purchaser? ___ Yes ___ No

22. Do you retrieve the parking pass, should your company issue them? ___ Yes ___ No

23. Do you cancel security codes used by the employee to get into the building, if your organization uses them? ___ Yes ___ No

24. Is employee picking up mail at the post office for the company? If so, do you get

the key back and notify the post office?
_____ Yes _____ No

25. Have you retrieved all keys the employee might have to desks? _____ Yes _____ No

26. Have you retrieved all keys to filing cabinets? _____ Yes _____ No

27. Have you retrieved all keys to any closets, especially if you have one containing pre-printed check stock? _____ Yes _____ No

28. If the departing employee handled petty cash, have you reconciled the box, before the employee leaves? _____ Yes _____ No

A **Discussion of the Best Practice Responses for the Checklist for Employee Departures**

While the correct response for all these issues is yes, it is not always obvious why these tasks need to be completed. Let's take a look at the reasoning behind the best practice responses.

1. You'd think retrieving all credit cards (T&E, p-card, fuel, one card) before the employee leaves would be a no-brainer, but surprisingly, it often doesn't happen. Getting the card back is the first step to ensuring the card is not used intentionally or by accident by the employee after he or she has left the organization.

2. By immediately notifying the card issuing bank to cancel the credit cards, you ensure no games will be played. An unscrupulous employee will simply write

down the pertinent information and use it for online purchases. Thus, it is critical that the card be canceled with the bank.

3. Similarly, by immediately notifying the bank to cancel any signing authorizations of departing employees for either paper checks or electronic payments, you eliminate any game playing on the part of a devious employee.

4. Retrieving the key to the building, if employees have them, not only protects you against game playing, it gives you a key for a new employee.

5. Retrieving all ID badges makes it difficult for an employee to get back into the building when they don't belong there.

6. Cutting off system access, including windows login on desktops makes it impossible for an ex-employee to play games with your data or look at company information to share with competitors— and yes, that occasionally happens.

7. By deactivating the employee in the master vendor file if they are included for expense reimbursement purposes makes it impossible for them to submit an expense report after they've left.

8. Request all outstanding expense reports, as soon as you know the employee is leaving so there is no reason to leave access to the expense reporting system once they are gone.

9. Request repayment of all outstanding travel advances, if your organization gives them before the employee leaves as that is when you have the most leverage. Once the employee is gone, it will be next to impossible to get the advance repaid.

10. Cancel all subscriptions (both print and online) requesting a refund for the unused amount as the organization is no longer responsible for the subscription nor will it get any benefit from it. Too often these just languish with no one reading the publication and hence, no benefit to the organization for the money spent.

11. Even more expensive than regular subscriptions are those to specialized databases. By requesting a refund for the unused amount, you help preserve the bottom line. (Note: Some organizations simply transfer these to the employee taking on the departing employee's responsibilities)

12. By addressing the issue of the telephone line, either returning the number to the telecom company or turning it over to someone else to handle any incoming calls, there is no waste.

13. Employees should not have access to their corporate e-mail accounts unless special provisions have been made. The employee's email accounts terminated or assigned to be read by someone else so

the employee cannot appear to be still employed by the organization.

14. If the e-mail account is assigned to someone else, the password should be changed. This will often be done if messages regarding company business continue to be sent to this e-mail address. This is just one more reason why invoices should not be sent to individual's e-mail addresses.

15. Likewise, ex-employee should not have access to their company's voice mail account. It should be terminated or assigned to be handled by someone else, especially if calls regarding company business are likely to come in on that line.

16. If the voice mail account is assigned to someone else, change the password so the ex-employee cannot access it.

17. Make sure you have a complete list of what employee is doing. Often employees perform tasks that are not included in the policy and procedures manual. These tend to evolve over time. This might be a good time to either update the policy manual and get them included or eliminate those tasks from the workflow.

18. Retrieve any laptop or cell phone or other equipment owned by the company but used by the employee. This is important so they can either be destroyed or given to someone else. Too often, people think the computer is old and why not let the

ex-employee have it as it has little intrinsic value. This misses the point. The real value is the information and access stored on the machine.

19. Don't forget to recover other company belongings such as manuals etc. New employees might make good use of them and you don't want corporate information floating around.

20. Make sure you have a current address for the employee. This is especially important if they are moving. For with this information you'll have fewer last checks going un-cashed and becoming unclaimed property.

21. If the employee is an authorized purchaser, contact suppliers and vendors to remove employee as authorized purchaser so they can't order items you neither want nor need.

22. Reclaim the parking pass, should your company issue them so ex-employees don't take up valuable parking spaces should they visit.

23. Cancel security codes used by the employee to get into the building, if your organization uses them so if an ex-employee wants to visit, they go through security just like all other non-employees.

24. If the employee picks up mail at the post office for the company, get the key back for the box and notify the post office. You'll need to give the key to whoever assumes this responsibility.

25. Get all keys the employee might have to employees' desks back as whoever is assigned to the desk will need it. Otherwise, you'll end up having to have the lock on the desk jimmied and a new key made.

26. Likewise, get all keys to filing cabinets back as the ex-employee has no need for them and whoever takes on their responsibilities does.

27. It is especially important to get all keys to any closets back, especially if you have one containing pre-printed check stock/

28. If the departing employee handled petty cash, reconcile the box, ideally before the employee leaves. If there is a discrepancy, you can resolve it and whoever takes on the box, takes it on with a clean slate. Of course, an even better idea is to simply get rid of petty cash.

New Terminology in Accounts Payable: BYOD. The first time I saw BYOD in a business article, I did a double take. Then I read on and realized I had been mistaken. As you probably are aware, many professionals are buying Smartphones and tablets for personal use. The term "devices" seems to be evolving to cover both of these items. Many buying these devices are bringing them to work to help with their day-to-day work processes.

Hence, the evolution of the term BYOD or "bring your own device."

Readers should note that there has been a good deal of controversy over this practice. The concern revolves around the use of these devices to assist in banking transactions and the potential lack of security protocols on the devices. The concern is that use of a device without the proper anti-virus/fraud software might make it easier for a crook to enact a takeover of the company's bank account

Short Regulatory Issues

• **IRS Continues March towards Paperless Filing.** The Electronic Tax Administration Advisory Committee (ETAAC) presented its 2013 Annual Report to Congress. The 15-member committee provides an organized public forum for discussion of electronic tax administration issues and the overriding goal that paperless filing should be the preferred and most-convenient method of filing tax and information returns. The report is the result of research and analysis as well as meetings with senior IRS executives. Included in its lists of recommendations was one that would provide incentives for e-filing employment tax returns.

• **Draft Form 1042-S.** The IRS released draft 1042-S. It includes the new reporting requirements imposed by FATCA and the reciprocal Intergovernmental Agreements (IGAs) that U.S. Treasury has been signing to implement FATCA in certain jurisdictions. The Form 1042-S has undergone substantial changes. You can view the draft of the form using the link at the end of this piece. However, please keep in mind it is a draft and is subject to change. http://www.irs.gov/pub/irs-dft/f1042s--dft.pdf

• **Determining Nexus in a State**. It's WAY more complicated than what you think, writes Jim Frazier on his blog. As some readers might be aware, Jim goes by the moniker The Sales Tax Guy and speaks regularly for AP Now on Sales and Use Tax issues. It's not just a matter of having an office there, he points out. There are some very surprising ways that you can have nexus in a state.

He notes that "Things change. The company might not have nexus today. But all it takes is for marketing to assign a sales person to regularly visit the state and you suddenly have nexus. Moreover the states have been getting more aggressive in this area. The emergence of the concepts of click-through nexus and affiliate nexus have changed the sale-and- use-tax landscape. In growing numbers, states have been successful in pushing through these concepts. Most notably, Amazon appears to have stopped fighting the states on these issues.

Short Tips Tactics & Strategies

• **Policy and Procedures Manual Updates**

While every reader probably knows their policy and procedures manual should be updated on a regular basis, and most mean to do just that, sometimes the project falls through the cracks. That's because it always seems like you updated the policy only yesterday.

Many are horrified to find out that when they check, it's actually been two or three years since anyone's looked at the manual. And, a lot can change in that period of time. One easy way to eliminate this problem and take the guess work out of the process is to date policy updates right on the cover of the policy and procedures manual. That eliminates any guessing. By the way, this will also work with your travel policy.

• **Who can approve what?** Do your processors really know who can approve what invoices? And, if so, how do you know? Is it just how things have evolved? Unfortunately, in many organizations, this is precisely how the process works. There is no accountability for authorization of approval levels.

Accountability ensures that your processors review, and approve invoices for payment based on signed agreements, contract terms, and purchase orders. It also means they have some direction on how can authorize what. Best practice organizations review and update signature authorizations periodically. The authorizations should come from the Board of Directors. Those authorizations can be further sub-delegated, but it should be done in writing.

• **Avoid A Tax Reporting Quagmire.** One of the issues companies sometimes face when work is performed by vendors located in another country is that of tax reporting. Sometimes it is not clear where the work was performed.

Request that foreign vendors doing work for your company outside the confines of the United States indicate that on their invoices. Request that invoices for services performed outside the United States expressly state that fact. Ask that they specify the city and country where the services were performed. For example, the invoice might state, "All services related to this invoice were performed outside the United States in [city] and [country].

• **Fraudsters Continue to Work around Banking Controls**. Did you know that a current method of counterfeiting is to chemically wash the ink off a $5 bill and use a color copier to print a larger denomination onto it? Because the fake bill is made of authentic paper, the counterfeit currency is more difficult to detect..

• **A Policy of Zero Tolerance**. AP Now has long recommended that organizations institute a policy of zero tolerance when it comes to fraud or other unethical behavior. This should come from the top of the organization and be included in the travel policy, the employee handbook and any other documents that might address the issue.

There is a real benefit to adopting such a policy. Experts indicate that employees who sign a company's written policy communicating a zero tolerance are 70 percent less likely to steal. The policy works as a strong deterrent.

Readers should note that if they have a p-card program, they can achieve a similar result by requiring cardholders to sign an agreement before they are given the card. The agreement should stipulate among other things that the cardholder understands that he or she can be terminated if they use the card inappropriately.

• **Old Controls that No Longer Work**. As the accounts payable function evolves, some of the old practices we used to rely on no longer work. Here are a few:

- ✓ Thinking only paying from an original invoice will protect you from duplicate payments
- ✓ Never paying from a fax
- ✓ Relying on boarding pass as proof trip was taken
- ✓ Putting forms for vendors on your website

Information about the monthly Accounts Payable Now & Tomorrow newsletter can be found at http://ap-now.com/subscribe.html

ABOUT THE AUTHOR

Mary S. Schaeffer, AP Now's publisher and editorial director, is a nationally recognized accounts payable expert. She is the author of over 15 business books, most focused on accounts payable issues, as well as a monthly newsletter and a free weekly e-zine.

Before turning to writing and consulting she worked in the corporate world as an Assistant Treasurer for the Equitable Life Assurance Society, a Financial Risk Manager for O&Y and a Corporate Cash Manager for Continental Grain.

She is a frequent speaker at industry conferences, one-day seminars and online events. She is also the creator of the IFO's Accounts Payable Innovation Certificate program and a number of CPE self-study courses for CPAs.

She speaks regularly at industry events, one-day seminars, conferences and online events. She has an MBA in Finance and a BS in Mathematics.

For additional information go to:
http://ap-now.com/expertise.html

ABOUT THE AP NOW

AP Now is the leading source of accounts payable information for the business and finance community. It offers a host of products and services designed to advance your department, your company, and your career. These include:

- ✓ E-AP News weekly ezine (complimentary)
- ✓ Accounts Payable Now & Tomorrow Newsletter (monthly fee-based publication delivered by e-mail)
- ✓ Webinars/teleconferences
- ✓ Seminars
- ✓ CDs
- ✓ Special Reports
- ✓ Blog
- ✓ Consulting services
- ✓ Customized Training (including FCPA)
- ✓ Duplicate Payment Resource Center (complimentary)

- For additional information go to www.ap-now.com

- For additional information about AP Now's free weekly e-zine focused on all issues related to accounts payable, go to http://ap-now.com/ezinesignup.html

www.ingramcontent.com/pod-product-compliance
Lightning Source LLC
Chambersburg PA
CBHW070408200326
41518CB00011B/2107